The Ang Book Of Light

ALAN Q. FRAZÃO

DEDICATION

Dedicated to God, The Angels and Archangels, My Inner-being, and all people that in someway helped me in my spiritual path.

CONTENTS

3

ACKNOWLEDGMENTS

Thank you God, Archangel Michael, and all other angels and archangels for letting me stand in my own power. Knowing that I create my own life, that I am the heir of all love, peace, money, etc that I may wish because God responds to my faith bringing to me all my needs. Thank you so much!

1 YOU ARE A MAGICAL BEING

You are a magical being that creates your reality. Everything is vibration which means you are always attracting things that are vibrating in the same way that you do. All situations, people, and circunstances that comes to your life is just because you invite it with your energy, your thoughts, your emotions. So to get what you want in life you just have to switch your point of attraction to a new place where your vibration is in sintony with heaven's will for you.

What you feel is what must determine what you are attraction to your life. If most of the time you feel joyfull, happy, gratefull and abundant probably you are getting more and more reasons to feel the same again.
But if the majority of the time you feel unhappy, anger, empty or depressed then probably you are attraction more reasons to feel the same again too.

It's heaven's desire that you have all the peace, love, prosperity, health and much more that you wish. But there's this spiritual law that says that you only gets what you are vibrating so here in this book you will learn not only to use your own vibrational power to attract what you want but also will get the help of the angels and archangels, candles, crystals, enchantments and much more that will add power to your spells and your ownself.

Putting into practice the spells here you will be invoking the power of heaven to give you all that is your divine inheritance as a child of God.

Say To Yourself now:

" I deserve all the money, peace, love, friendships and so on I wish for my life because is God's promisse to me to take care of all my needs and all I need to do is to switch my vibration to matches God's will for me that is my highest good!"

2 THE LUNAR CYCLES

new moon : It's the perfect time to call your angels, visualize, or cast a spell for new relationships, a new carrear, or bring new ideas and habits into your life.

Waxing (or growing) moon: Time to empower yourself, to work into your faith, to become more strengh, and making a relationship you are already into more stronger , with more love and confidence.

Waning (Or Shrinking) Moon: time to get over low energies, toxic thoughts, and clear your energy calling for archangel michael to detox you, and chamuel to help you to have higher patterns of thoughts. clear your space from old objects, job, relationships etc that are not surving your highest good.

Full Moon : Amazing for love spells. Visualize a romantic relationship, cast a romance spell with a pink candle, or call archangel chamuel for help to bring you your soulmate. Time when you are more aware of your thoughts and emotions, and that you feel your emotions multiplied (so if you have being having positive thoughts you probably will feel wonderfull, if you have being having negative thoughts you may feel depressed). So it's perfect to notice what you have being attracting into your life and take time to visualize what you want, make a list of gratitude, do a spell for more faith and confidence, or whatever you feel guided to, even if you don't feel the in the mood to do it.
It's a life changing moment if you really take time to have the most positive thoughts about each area of your life. Time for instant manifestations!

Dark Moon: Time to reflect about what you want, to take time alone, to make a list of desires, to relax and enjoy with no precupation. You will clear decide what you want and than use your power to manifest in the next new moon or full moon to attract miracles to your life. Just think about "what I most want in life?". Perfect time to create spells you will use in the other phases of the moon.

3 THE DAYS OF THE WEEK

Sunday: Divine power, time to cast spells for healing and to tranquility, solar energy.
Archangels to invoke : Raphael & Jophiel

Monday: Moon energy for beginnings and psychic powers
Archangel to invoke : Haniel

Tuesday: energy for faith, courage, and physical strength
Archangels to invoke : Michael & Raphael

Wednesday: Time to learn, teach and communicate
Archangels to invoke : Ariel, Uriel & Gabriel

Thursday: wealth, luck, & materialism
Archangel to invoke : Ariel

Friday: Energy for love, art & music
Archangel to invoke : Chamuel , also call the romance angels

Saturday: Time to find the solution of a problem / to finish projects
Archagel to invoke : Jeremiel

4 THE SUN AND IT'S EFFECT IN THE SPELLS

The sun can enhance the power of your spells just like the moon is also associate with divine magic.

See bellow the effect of each moment of the sun:

Dawn Sun
The morning sun represents the miracle of life and the divine. It's perfect to be outdoor casting any spell for new beginners, prosperity and power. It's considered the most powerfull sun time to cast your spells.

Midday Sun
It's very powerfull because it's associated with the magical number 12. And it's the opposite of the midnight moon that is also a magical time. It's perfect for when you need a boost of your energy, like dealing with prosperity or a business, or getting over grief.

Colors associated with the Sun
· White
· Red
· Corn Yellow
· Gold
· Blue (Representing The Sky)

Crystals For Sun Rituals
· Green Gemstones (especially emerald and jade)
· Amber and Yellow Gems (such as sapphires)

5 MY SOULMATE SPELL

Best time to cast the spell:
Thursday of friday

If you want to dream about your soulmate and attract this person into your life this is the spell.

It's said that when you dream about your soulmate this person is almost comming into your life.

So light a floral incense, do a few deep breaths, and listen to your favorite love song.

As you do that think about 3 , 7, or more feelings you would have with your soulmate.
(like love, secure, happiness, peace, joy...)

then in a pink or red piece of paper write down:
"my soulmate"
and say to your angels
"please archangel chamuel and my guardian angels, bring me my soulmate"

put the paper inside your pillow and leave it there until you dream about your soulmate. But trust this to happen soon or in divine time.

6 ALWAYS YOUNG SPELL

In the morning, at least 1 day a week, prepare an apple juice and touching the cup call archangel Jophiel, the fitness angels, and the beauty angels to be always next to you rejuvenating your body, mind, and soul.

Meaning they will help your cells to work properly, help you to make good choises about exercises and diet, and also making you have positive thoughts that will give a boost to your beauty and Youth .

They can really make you beautiful inside and out.

After praying to them still holding the touching or holding the cup chant:
The beauty in me
everybody will see
I am free to always shine
always young I will be
I now have a perfect young body and a beautiful soul!"

Now hold to that feeling knowing that you born to shine. Trust your angels to make your cells to work in your best benefit and also to help you make better choises in your life. You are safe and you are beautiful!

7 ATTRACT A NEW HOME SPELL

When to cast the spell:
Thursday Evening

light a sandalwood incense, and think about how would be your perfect home. Draw it in a piece of paper. Have fun with it making something beautiful and that you really appreciates. Then, write down at least 7 things about your new home.

Ex.: In my home there's 3 bedrooms, a big garden, it's near the shopping mall, etc.

After using your imagination and focus to drawn your home and list how you would like it to be, chant:

"Ariel come to me now
My new home I want now
It's so beautiful
and so conforting
Now I receive from heaven my new home"

Then simple hold the feeling of fun, amazement, and high expectation you had when drawning your new home. Feel as already having it.

8 BRING HAPPINESS TO MY LIFE SPELL

If you need to feel more happiness or more excited about life this is a wonderfull spell.

Take a shower and imagine that you are washing away all negative thoughts and emotions. There's a golden light that is flowing with the water and cleaning you for all energy that is not surving you.

Now put coloured clothing (yellow is very good to represent happiness) or your favorite clothes.

Go to another place where you feel confortable, light a yellow candle and drawn the sun in a piece of paper. Below this sun write 3 situations that you was very happy like a day you went out with friends to the beach, our that you watched your favorite movie, or the trip you had. Then, write 3 situations you would like to happen to you asking your angels to make it true.

It would be like this:

(the image of the sun goes here)

Happy now   Intentions of happiness
 (things that already happened   (your desires for the near future)
that made you feel happy)

Now chant:
"angels of happiness comes to me now
happiness is heaven's vow
my desires will come true
the unhappiness is undone
Now only happiness, fun and joy sorrounds me and the situations in my

life!"

Now trust the angels and archangels that all will be well for you, that you are safe, and already for the fun life have for you! Say to them "Thank you angels and archangels for making my life an amazing adventure" , and trust it to be true!

9 BRING THIS PERSON BACK INTO MY LIFE SPELL

Chant this spell you there's someone from your past that you lose contact you would like to see back into your life.

Light a pink candle, a white and yellow candle together.

That represents the love and appreciation you have for this person,

the white candle represents the relief of having this person back into your life and the yellow represents the joy you both had together.

Now invoke the presence of archangel's chamuel and raguel. And think about some of the moments you had with this person. The places you went together, the things you done, and the feeling of being together.

Then, imagine having this person back into your life holding that same feeling you used to have when near this person. What you are doing? Where you both are? feel it.

And finally chant:

By the power of three
we are near
our friendship (or love) is back
come to me here
now you returned to me!"

Now simple trust your angels to bring this person back to your life.

10 CHANNEL OF THE DIVINE SPELL

If you want to feel more confident about your power to listen to the angels, to attract your desires, or anyone spiritual stuff do this spell to increase your confidence into your power.

Holding a aquamarine stone call archangel Haniel, imagine there's a mix of gold and purple light sorrounding you. The golden light represents your power, the purple light the divine force and spiritual evolution.

Now as you visualize it think about at least one spiritual experience you had, like having an answered prayer, or attraction something you wanted. If you don't remember or think you never had one just ask the angels to give it to you in the near future.

And then chant:

"Inside me divine magic lives

I am the likeness and image of God

with his power, wisdom and love

I know truly know and and trust it

I am a hundred percent capable to talk to the angels, attract my desires, and life a spiritual life easily. Thank you"

Now put your aquamarine stone near your bed and ask your angels to appear to you in your dreams bringing messages and direction for your spiritual life. But most of all know now and forever that you truly are 100% powerfull to create your reality and connect with the angels. Just trust and listen.

11 COLORS OF JOY SPELL

If you feel you need a boost of energy, happiness, and balance into your life do this spell to really feel more excited about life.

Call archangel Ariel, Jophiel, and Michael to yourside.

Now imagine Archangel Michael sending you his royal purple light, it's energizing you with the divine energy of creativity and integrity.

then, imagine Archangel Jophiel sending you a yellow light it's the energy of joy, positive thoughts, and excitment.

And then imagine Ariel sending you a red light it's the energy of excitment for your passions, your desires, and projects.

Imagine this as much time you want absorving this energy of power.

After finish just keep going in the direction of your desires feeling with more ideas, joy, and passion.

You can also pray to your angels "please give me wonderfull ideas, positive thoughts, and passion for life", they will hear and help you with this. Their help will come with instant results and also with guidance.

12 CHANNEL OF THE DIVINE SPELL

If you want to feel more confident about your power to listen to the angels, to attract your desires, or anyone spiritual stuff do this spell to increase your confidence into your power.

Holding a aquamarine stone call archangel Haniel, imagine there's a mix of gold and purple light sorrounding you. The golden light represents your power, the purple light the divine force and spiritual evolution.

Now as you visualize it think about at least one spiritual experience you had, like having an answered prayer, or attraction something you wanted. If you don't remember or think you never had one just ask the angels to give it to you in the near future.

And then chant:

"Inside me divine magic lives

I am the likeness and image of God

with his power, wisdom and love

I know truly know and and trust it

I am a hundred percent capable to talk to the angels, attract my desires, and life a spiritual life easily. Thank you"

13 FLY HIGH SPELL

If you want to make your life go to a next level it's the spell for you.

Call archangel michael, ariel, and chamuel to be with you.

Then in a piece of paper with the color of what you most desire

love = pink

money = green

peace = white

happiness = yellow

write what changes you want to see in your life. Like having a new romantic partnet, getting a new job, or anything. Write all you want even if they are not related wishes.

Now in a full moon night chant this holding the paper:

"Angels of the wishes coming true

my time of suffering is overdue

My wishes are true now

because heaven here me now

The angels receive and answer my wishes now"

Now simple tear the paper or burn it. And blow it away or throw the ashes away.

14 FORGET MY EX SPELL

Best time to do this spell:

in a waning moon

If someone hurt you but you still cannot forget this person and go on with your life that's a good spell for you.

Call archangel michael and raphael, light 2 white candles, and a red candle.

the 2 white candles is to bring peace for you both

the red candle is to make you stronger

So now ask archangel michael to vanish away all cords between you and this person. Say that you are willing to forgive but also willing to forget him. Also ask Raphael to set you free from any pain you still feel about this relationship.

In a piece of paper write the person's name , and burn it while you chant:

"(person's name) you are cast out of my memory now

 because full peace is heaven's vow

I now am complete free

to live the life I should be

So let it be!"

Now trust this person will not appear any more into your mind, and all feelings and thoughts about her is vanish from your mind. The angels are totally available to help you to attract a even better person into your life to make you really happy, more than in any other relationship. Trust heaven.

15 FRIENDSHIP RECONCILIATION SPELL

light 2 white candles, invoke archangel raguel (call mentally or aloud), and think about 3 situations and 3 qualities of your friend. (Or more)

Now chat this:

"With you I make peace

our friendship never dies

true friends are heaven's prize

Raguel is now with us

we have a peacefull and loving friendship together"

Now just hold the feeling of being in peace and truly loving your friend forgiving the past and being open for a new beggining.

16 HEALTHY AND HAPPY SPELL

If you want to feel more healthy and more happy try this spell.

Wake up on the morning and drink a glass of water (or even more if you want).

Then, go outside and feel the sunbeams touching your body.

Hold a Citrine stone to energise it your sun energy.

And think about 3 or 7 reasons (or more) you have to be happy in your life.

It can be simple things like "the water I drink, or the food I eat", or whatever you feel gratefull.

Stand in this place feeling the emotion of happiness and gratetude about the things that came into your mind, no matter how you think it's so small or big, just be gratefull. Do it during 5 or 10 minutes feeling also the sumbeams touching your skin.

And after it chant:

"My body is a temple of happiness

My soul is a temple for joy

Thank you michael for standing near me

and for unhappiness set me free

I am gratefull, happy, and healthy now!"

Now leave the citrine stone with you and hold it anytime you want to feel more happiness or to pray for joy. Or simple leave it absorving the sun's energy during the day.

17 INVISIBILITY SPELL

If you don't want to be noticed by people around you, or want to feel more safe in a situation where not being seen would feel more confortable do this spell.

Call archangel michael (mentally or aloud) and visualize a royal purple or blue light (his color) extracting your colors or your body. It's like a tornado above you extracting all your physical form. You don't have to visualize it for so long, just for a few seconds or as much you feel confortable , and get the feeling of being invisible.

So now people around you will more difficult notice your presence, or will not even notice at all.

It's good when you just want to be alone and not disturbed even with other people around you.

18 LOTERRY WINNER SPELL

Best time to cast the spell:

monday night at seven o'clock

Pick a dollar bill of any value or a another thing that represents money , luck or prosperity to you. Just remember it can not be something you are going to spend, give to another person, or throw away. So it have to be something you really like and that will remain with you.

You can also drawn a beautiful star in a piece of paper, cut out, and use it to this spell.

Pick you object and touching it think about 7 times you spent money, bought something, or gained something in your life.

As you do this, or after , chant:

"Angels of prosperity come to me now

Angels of abundance show me heaven's fortune

I am sorround with luck now

Money money money in my way is heaven's vow

I am prosperous and lucky!"

Now, if you can write the lucky numbers 7,9, and 12 inside your object, star , or money.

* probably you can't write in your money, because of your country's law. So just say the numbers as you touch the money.

Then, holding the object ask the angels to guide you to the correct loterry numbers. And write what came into your mind. If it don't happen in the first moment, don't lose your faith, just remember the angels have many other ways to provide you the money you need that can be with a new job, fullfilling your life's purpose, and even in miraculous ways. So now your needs are supplied as long you ask for help and trust.

19 MAKE A WISH SPELL

Best time for this spell:

Evening of a new moon

Imagine a golden light comming from the sky into you, fullfilling all your body.

It's God's power, your own consciousness of being one with God and able to create your own reality. So receive this energy as you say:

"I am one with my creator. He gave me the power to create my own reality. And so it is"

Now put your index finger in one of the names bellow of the archangels and their blessings.

Imagine part of this golden light you received going into this words you put your finger, you are charging it with your magical power.

now chant:

"My wish come true

It's God's Will

And that's real

I now receive my blessing

My desire is a reality!"

Now pick a piece of paper and put inside the book with your wish written on it and leave it there for 24 hours or as much time you want.

Raphael   Michael   Ariel

(health)   (protection)   (money)

Haniel   Chamuel   Raguel

(Psychic Power)   (Love)   (Friendships)

20 MIRROR MIRROR SPELL

Call archangel jophiel the archangel of beauty to your side. Do this spell if you want to be and feel more beautiful inside and out.

Doing the spell:

Get a mirror, look at your face on it, and think about at least 3 things you like about yourself. If you are with low self-esteem just think about anything you appreciate about yourself. The 3 things can be about your personality, your body, or behaviors.

Like : "I appreciate being a so loving person" or "I appreciate my eyes"

Now still looking at the mirror chant:

"Archangel Jophiel that sees heaven in me

my trueself let me be

beautiful inside and out

as heaven sees me I see now

I am a beautiful person in my soul and body!"

Now just try to hold the feeling of appreciating yourself during the day, listing things you like about yourself. If need help call Jophiel to also help you seeing the beauty in yourself.

21 MONEY MAGNET SPELL

Get a 3 coins of any value and put inside a glass of water.

Now touching the glass take some time to think about what you want to buy with the money you desire, and what's the feeling of having it.

Also think about how much love you would feel for the money if you could buy all this things.

Then still touching the glass of water say:

"Archangel Michael and Ariel

raise my vibration now

let me prosper

and fullfill my dreams

Thank you for my perfect financial life"

Now pick the coins and put in your wallet, pocket, or whatever you want. Or in a special place in your home. It's now magnetized with the energy of prosperity, also you are too.

Going out with the coins with you will bring luck, more money, and opportunities.

22 MY LOVE BACK SPELL

When to cast the spell:

8 o'clock in the evening

light 2 white candles, take a few deep breaths, and think about something that makes you feel very calm, peacefull, and enlighted. Like maybe spending the day in a beach, in a garden, or looking to the moon.

After doing this for a few minutes hold a picture of your lover and chant:

"between me and you

only love will be

that's my desire

our hearts are full of fire

we have peace and love with each other now"

say the person's name 3 times and then put his/her picture in your heart and say this sentences:

"I am sorry. I appreciate you. I am gratefull. I love you"

Now mantein this feeling of love, peace, and appreciation between you both. Knowing that the best for both of you will happen. And that now the vibrational energy between you and him is clear (in a place of peace and love).

23 MY LUCK ANGEL NUMBER SPELL

Write in a piece of paper all the numbers from 0 to 9.

Write the same numbers 3 times.

And then cut each of the numbers and put into a bag.

Visualize what you want to see manifested in your life. Think about your desires during 3 , 7, 12 or more minutes and ask your angels to manifest them into reality to you. Also ask them to give you your luck angel number.

Then put 3 numbers from the bag and put them together in other. That's your lucky number for you to think when you need more strengh and faith to go on.

to get the meaning of the angel number you got go to :

http://easycalculation.com/other/fun/angel-number-calculator.php

or read doreen virtue's book angel numbers.

Now simple tear the paper or burn it. And blow it away or throw the ashes away.

24 MY SOULMATE SPELL

Best time to cast the spell:

Thursday of friday

If you want to dream about your soulmate and attract this person into your life this is the spell.

It's said that when you dream about your soulmate this person is almost comming into your life.

So light a floral incense, do a few deep breaths, and listen to your favorite love song.

as you do that think about 3 , 7, or more feelings you would have with your soulmate.

(like love, secure, happiness, peace, joy...)

then in a pink or red piece of paper write down:

"my soulmate"

and say to your angels

"please archangel chamuel and my guardian angels, bring me my soulmate"

put the paper inside your pillow and leave it there until you dream about your soulmate. But trust this to happen soon or in divine time.

25 MY TRUE LOVE IN THE MOON LIGHT

Hold a pink quartzo with you in a day of full moon. Go outside and look to the moon as you think about the qualities in a partner. How he would treat you, what's his behaviors, and how you feel near him. Take at least 1 or 2 minutes.

Then chant :

"My true love I can see

this moon light is showing me

love is real and accessible

and it's available for me now

Thank you heaven for my perfect partner"

Now go when you go to sleep put the crystal near your bed. (in a table for example)

You can also put your pink quartzo in your pocket, wallet, or purse and hold it with you every place you go with the energy of love.

26 NEW JOB, NEW BOSS

If you are angry with your boss that don't treat well it's time to use your inner-power to manifest a new one.

Get a piece of paper and write in it the reasons why you want a new job, don't put it in negative sentences, instead say it in the most positive ways.

Like:

If what you think is "my boss don't treat me well", write "I want a boss that treats me well"

Or if what you think is "I don't receive a good salary" write "I want to be well-paid"

at the end of your text about what you want you probably will have something like this:

"I want a boss that treats me well, with love and respect. I also want to be well-paid and feel good in the environment I work with loving and gentle people working with me. "

Write everything that comes to your mind in a positive pespective.

Then drop golden gritter in the paper as you say:

"My new job I receive

thank you michael, thank you ariel

In heaven's help I believe

I am now guided and safe

Thank you angels for my new dream job"

Now just believe the angels received your intentions and it's answered.

27 NICE DREAMS SPELL

If you have nightmares it's a good thing to call archangel michael and your dream guide to change it.

Before sleep imagine a royal blue or puble buble light around you. (it's michael energy)

Call archangel michael and your dream guide and chant:

"sweet dreams I will have

positive aspects to live

a happy life to feel

come to me now michael, come to me now dream guide

only benefitial dreams I will have!"

Now go to sleep in peace knowing that they hearded your intention.

28 PASS EXAM SPELL

Before sleep hold a fluorite stone and imagine your sleep getting a good grade in your exam. Imagine how happy and excited you will feel, and how proud of yourself.

Now after sleep study the most important topics of your exam at least for sometime. And then put the notebook or a resume of the content of your books under your pillow.

And pray to your angels and the archangels (especially Uriel) that as you sleep you will absorve from the book all you need to know for the exam.

Please remember to really study for your exame, but doing this spell you will feel more confidence, peacefull, and also the archangels will really be with you during the exam to help you remeber things easily. So it's to boost your confidence and also get some help from the angels but in a deserve way because they know you studied or at least they can help you because they know if you trully didn't had the time or energy to study.

29 SET ME FREE SPELL

If you feel someone is sending you hash/negative energy with their intentions or physical actions. Use this spell to breack the "hex" or to stop this person to make any harm to you.

Time to cast the spell:

Midnight on a saturday

In a yellow piece of paper write down the name of the person how is harming you in a physical or spiritual way. If you don't know the name just write "person who is harming me"

Using a pink pen circle the person's name. You are drawning a circle of protection to this person not harm you.

And chant with the angels:

"Archangel michael with your protection

set me free of this person of my objection

If not with love this person will not be able to be near me

because only love can get next to me

this spell now sets me free, only love sorrounds me"

Now if you want you can burn this paper representing your desire getting to heaven. Or simple put it in a box or another place. Knowing that now that you asked the angels are around you letting only love to get your way. They can never interfere in other people's free will, but they can guide you and protect you from their behaviors.

30 SPEAK YOUR TRUTH SPELL

Holding a aquamarine stone think about who believe yourself to be. Think about your desires, projects, personality, and especially what you have not being able to show people right now, maybe you need to be courageous to go out of your spiritual closet, or to tell your parents what carrear you really would like to follow, and to be honest with your friends about your favorite stuff instead of allowing them to shape your personality.

If you want write what's these things you would like people to know without having to hide yourself anymore. When writing just leave the crystal near you.

Then put a very calm song you like, maybe a new age song and relax. (you can also do this when you are still making your list). At this time call michael and ariel to your side and chant:

"I am a warrior of God

I am accepted by him for who-I-am

I was made to shine with my trueself

that's the way to fullfill God's destiny for me

I now open myself to be my trueself, and that's God's will for me!"

Now burn this paper in a white candle and ask the angels to bring peace and courage to you to be who-God-made-you-to-be. To show your true intentions and dreams. It's divine correct and acceptable, it's what God and angels wants for you. You are safe and protected by them.

Also bring the crystal with you whatever you go and need more courage to speak your truth.

31 SPELL FOR BEING LOVED AND SUCCESSFUL

Magical Object To use:

- 1 mirror

Instructions:

Take a shower and during the shower call archangel michael and raphael chanting:

"With this water that I can see

all bad energy get away from me

I only see the best in me

I am perfect right now and here

thank you angels because now I see myself as the perfect child of God that I Am"

Then take time to think for some minutes about the things you most love about your personality and body.

After doing it for at least 5 or 10 minutes be in front of the mirror and say:

"Inside my eyes I see the perfection of the inner being that I truly am" than smile or even laught at the mirror if you feel inspired to do it, and say:

"I am an example of happiness, self-confidence, and self-love to others"

to finish put your clothers and chant:

"The best in me is what I see

perfect love, perfect body, perfect soul

of my live I am in control

thank you God for who I am

and now the world if the mirror of the love I have inside for my ownself, I am loved."

Now live your life knowing that wherever you feel about yourself others will feel too, so always see you as fantastic.

32 TRUTH SPELL

If you want to discover the truth about a situation, or what someone is hiding you this is the spell for you.

Holding a moonstone, call archangel haniel to enhance your psychic powers and to show you the truth. Call archangel chamuel too. They them the situation you are living and why you want to know the truth, and how can it benefit you and others.

Now chat:

"I want now the truth revealed

all the secrets will be unsealed

help me angels to know now

what haven't being told

The truth sets me free now!"

So know just think about the feeling you would have knowing it, and hold yourself to that feeling, knowing that now things are getting orchestrated to reveal you the truth. Feel like already having this truth revealed with you.

33 VALENTINE'S CHOCOLATE PRESENT

If you are interested in someone in special you can also count on magic and angels to give that special help. Of course the angels can't go against other people's freewill, neither you can do this, but they can help the person to be more open to see your value, and if it's for the best benefit of both of you bring you together.

So buy a box of chocolate, and hold it with a pink ribbon.

after doing it imagine yourself sending love energy to this person, in your imagination the person is in a pink bubble of pure divine love. At the same time think about your qualities, of all you can offer to this person. And send him/her this information too with your intention.

Then chant holding the box of chocolate:

"Chamuel Archangel of love

let _____ be my true love

I beg you to bring him now

but just if it's meant to be and heaven's vow

thank you for bringing this person to me"

Now give the box of chocolate to the person you love being gratefull to heaven that if he/she will be of great value to you and vice versa this person will be your partner.

34 WISHING ON A STAR SPELL

Look for the britest star in the sky (or the one most calls your attention)

and take sometime to think what you would like to happen in your life

then ask ariel and michael to be with u in this moment

and chant:

"I wish on a star

heaven hear me now

let my desire be your vow

with the blessing of the archangels

I have want I want now"

Repeat this as many times as you want as you imagine the situation you would like to live, take at least one or two minutes visualizing or thinking about how would feel having your desire being truth in your life.